AIMING
FOR YOUR
NORTH
STAR

The 4 Phases to Reach Liftoff
for Your Growth Journey

MARIE-CLAUDE DESROSIERS

AIMING FOR YOUR NORTH STAR

Drive to Growth LLC
486 S. Ripley BLVD. Suite #313 • Alpena, MI 49707 • United States
www.drivetogrowth.com

Printed in the United States of America
First Printing, 2021

ISBN-10: 1-7369698-0-3
ISBN-13: 978-1-7369698-0-9
Ebook: 978-1-7369698-2-3

Library of Congress Control Number: 2021914348

Edited by The Editor Garden, LLC, www.editorgarden.com

Book Cover & Text Layout: Summer R. Morris
www.SumoDesignStudio.com

AIMING FOR YOUR NORTH STAR

To my dad, who was the first to see my potential and ignite my growth journey. To every dreamer brave enough to start their growth journey and aim for their best self.

CONTENTS

INTRODUCTION:
BE THE BEST YOU CAN BE!   1

PHASE 1:   SCAN YOUR SKY   7
SCAN #1:   SCAN YOUR INTERNAL FORCE   10
SCAN #2:   SCAN YOUR INTERNAL DIALOGUE   16
SCAN #3:   SCAN YOUR REACTIONS   23
SCAN #4:   SCAN YOUR EXCUSES   29

PHASE 2:   TEST YOUR POINT OF VIEW   35
POV #1:   CHART YOUR POINT OF VIEW   37
POV #2:   BLAST YOUR FEARS   42
POV #3:   PUSH PAST YOUR COMFORT ZONE   45
POV #4:   LEARN FROM YOUR MISTAKES   49

PHASE 3:   ACT TO REACH YOUR NORTH STAR   53
ACTION #1:   KNOW YOUR DESTINATION   56
ACTION #2:   SET YOUR VOYAGE   64
ACTION #3:   START YOUR ENGINE   68

PHASE 4:   REFLECT ON YOUR DESTINATION   77
REFLECT #1:   LOOK BACK AT THE EARTH   79
REFLECT #2:   SHOOT FOR THE STARS   84

CONCLUSION:
I BELIEVE YOU CAN REACH YOUR NORTH STAR!   89

ACKNOWLEDGMENTS   91

NOTES   93

APPENDIX   95

BE THE BEST
YOU CAN BE!

My personal growth journey started at age eleven during a family vacation in Northern Montreal. One afternoon, my dad and I decided to go to the hotel pool. I could hear laughter and splashing of water coming from the pool. At first glance, I saw two young children my age playing in the shallow end. I asked my dad, "Is it OK if I play with these kids?" My dad answered, "Sure." It took me a few seconds to realize they were not speaking French but English. I only spoke French. We would have to communicate through hand signals.

We played for fifteen to thirty minutes before my dad spoke English to my new friends and asked where they were from. I remember thinking, *Oh, my gosh! My dad speaks English!* I jumped with joy. My dad would be able to translate my questions. When

I asked my dad to tell me what my new friends were saying, he answered, "If you want to communicate with them, you need to learn English." *What?* I was so mad at him. During that emotional experience, I made the decision to learn English. I remember telling myself, *I will show you who is the better English speaker in the family*. At that moment, I felt the energy to embark on my first personal growth journey. I often reach inside myself to rekindle the spark of energy I gained that day, that driving force, to keep me going in times of adversity.

My encounter at the pool showed me an opportunity to grow I had never explored before. A new, controllable goal with the choice to pursue it or not. The powerless feeling of not communicating and connecting with others was stronger than the status quo of being unable to speak English. I wasn't afraid of failing or looking for excuses to disengage in my quest. Everything was crystal clear; I needed to learn English, period. A one-minute experience created a lifelong ambition. It started a transformation, a journey beyond my wildest dreams. Throughout my journey to learn English, themes emerged:

✦ My internal voice was negative. The first phrase that popped into my mind was, *I can't learn this; it's too hard.* Nobody around me was telling me that. I was my own worst enemy; I was limiting myself.

✦ Excuses were too numerous to count. My go-to excuse was, *I will speak English publicly when my French accent is gone.* I still have an accent to this day.

✦ Fear became paralyzing: *If I make a mistake, people will laugh at me.*

✦ Daily practice made a difference. Repeating new English words and phrases like a parrot made me better. During these practice sessions, I discovered that my persistence and focused dedication were my greatest strengths.

✦ Pushing beyond my comfort zone accelerated my learning. Asking my high school teacher to be part of a school trip to Winnipeg allowed me to see how far I could go. The experience made me realize that by fully immersing into an English-only environment, I would exponentially increase my knowledge.

✦ Accepting imperfections and learning from my mistakes helped me turn the corner in my growth. I learned to accept that I would speak English with some imperfections, and I used those imperfections and mistakes to learn and grow.

✦ Establishing a learning plan with my high school English teacher made me see the power of planning my growth journey.

✦ Listening to recordings of my discussions with my English teacher taught me the importance of looking back and extracting the lessons I learned.

Growth will always lead you to change your circumstances. The eleven-year-old girl that wanted to communicate with friends in a swimming pool ended up marrying a man who spoke only English, working full-time in English, and becoming a United States citizen. The journey forged my habits, developed critical behaviors, pushed me to action, and revealed the power of reflection in my personal growth journey.

My aspiration is clear and simple: candidly share my practices to help others reach their North Star. A North Star is a vision of your best self. It is the image, the unfulfilled potential, the next destination you strive to accomplish. Your North Star is the journey to be your best throughout life. Everyone has potential, and embracing the challenge to develop it is up to you. You control four factors to reach your North Star: your reaction to adversity, your behavior, how you make it happen, and how you extract lessons to set your next destination. Taking ownership of these four variables will make you what I call a *North Star Lifer*, a lifelong learner, or personal growth expert. You have the power to reach any version of your North Star.

Here are the four phases designed as a travel guide, a way to chart your journey to your North Star. The STAR model is:

1. Scan your sky: understand your strengths and your limiting stories.

2. Test your point of view: embrace critical behaviors that help you reach your goal.

3. Act to reach your North Star: execute your plan and fulfill your potential.

4. Reflect on your destination: evaluate your actions to set your next direction.

This method has generated immediate results for each goal I wanted to accomplish in my life. I will be honest with you; the road to my North Star looks more like a set of stairs than a straight line. That is fine. Incremental advancement, even in a zigzag pattern, helps us recognize progress. It keeps us motivated through our growth journeys. I hope this book enables you to execute all the goals you desire to achieve. Anything is possible.

At the end of each chapter, you will find plenty of space to write your thoughts. Some chapters include questions that you can answer to internalize specific insights. Let me mentor you and help you reach your North Star. Are you ready? Let's start your journey!

SCAN YOUR SKY

There were only a few things in my high school years that I knew about myself: I had a positive attitude, a curious mindset, and great determination once I set my mind to something. These attributes carried me through college and into a job a few months after graduation. In the first eight years of my adulthood, I enjoyed building my own life. I got a new car, found love, bought a house, and had my son. You could say that in my 20s, I laid the foundation for my family life. I felt blessed. At the beginning of my 30s, I wondered what I wanted to accomplish in the next decade. I realized I was not sure what I wanted to do. I searched for my next goal by asking five questions:

1. What am I good at?

2. What do I love to do?

3. Am I using my strengths at work?

4. How do I feel about my current job?

5. Why am I staying at that job?

After a few days of reflection, I identified the following observations for each question:

+ Strengths: I have a natural talent for teaching others. I am a fast learner. My level of energy and focus is high. I make quick decisions and execute them rapidly. I manage myself well.

+ Passions: I love learning new things, connecting the dots, and sharing my learnings with others. I am fulfilled when mentoring and coaching new team members.

+ Strengths at work: I use my levels of energy, focus, and decisiveness every day, but I'd like more opportunities to learn. I use half of my strengths at work.

+ Passion for work: I feel energized when teaching skills and helping employees manage their everyday work effectively. I do not have the chance to practice my passion regularly. I like my co-workers and the company, but I feel my potential is capped. I studied for four years in college to become a manager, and I am not using those skills.

✦ Why I stay: I am still happy at my job. I work the night shift, and it gives me more time with my son during the day. However, I cannot be a manager without regular managing experience. I have been turned down for promotions before, so I must be missing skills.

Looking at that list, I realized my reasons were based on false beliefs and driven by my lack of confidence. They were excuses for not pushing myself beyond my comfort zone. At that moment, I had a choice: continue with the status quo or reach for my potential. I wanted a career, not a job. I had to find a way to change my job and become the supervisor I believed I could be. But as soon as I made this decision, providence stepped in. My company lost a big contract and had to downsize. Since I was the last person in, I was laid off. I had no choice now. I could start searching for a new career. By understanding my strengths and interests before being laid off, I uncovered the direction I needed to take. My North Star was defined: be a supervisor. Within six weeks, I was hired as a production and laboratory supervisor.

Throughout my life, I had to redo this analysis. Understanding ourselves, our reactions, and mostly our excuses is essential to breaking through our comfort zone. To scan your sky, you need to learn the following:

1. Your interests and strengths

2. Your internal dialogue

3. Your reactions

4. Your excuses

In the next four sections, we will take a deeper look at the tools we can use to know ourselves better.

SCAN #1: SCAN YOUR INTERNAL FORCE

All of us were created with our own differences. We all have attributes that are unique to us. What makes you, you? To scan your sky, you need to first understand your internal forces. These internal forces are shown through personal strengths, life experience, and personality. Have you ever noticed that some tasks come easy to you, but for someone else it takes much longer? It is because you are executing one of your strengths. For example, one of my colleagues at the laboratory used to teach interns during the summer. She told me that she found no pleasure in it and was stressed. When my boss told me to take over the training for her, it was like a weight lifted off her shoulders. I love teaching others; it gives me great satisfaction and energy. Time flies when I am using one of my strengths.

When you dive into what you love, it is much easier to see potential growth opportunities. I call them your *growth zones*.

These growth zones can also be used to reveal your talents at work, thus benefiting your team and your company. In the example above, my colleague's gift was her ability to organize. Her method for ordering laboratory tests was the most efficient and rapid system for our technicians. By learning from her, I showed the interns the best method for success in their first week at work. By using each person's strengths, managers can create an environment where all employees feel valued.

I believe that focusing on your strengths reaps better results. Improving your strengths will be more impactful than working on your weaknesses. Since you already love your strengths, you have an interest in learning new things about them. This is true for me. My curiosity drives me to ask questions and look for better ways to be. For example, teaching with other people helped me improve my teaching style. The way my colleagues taught a topic, their engagement with the class, and the types of examples they would share gave me some of my biggest growth nuggets as a public speaker. It sounds like I had all my strengths figured out from the start, doesn't it? To be honest, it took me a long time to figure out my strengths and preferences. I still discover new insights about myself every year. You may be in the same situation right now, and that's perfectly fine. The search to know oneself is a lifelong journey. To learn more about your internal forces, you need to do the following:

1. Know your personality style

2. Find your specific strengths

3. See your internal force through others

To understand your personality style, I suggest taking *The Maxwell DISC Personality Indicator Report* assessment (for more information, visit www.drivetogrowth.com). When completed, you'll receive details on your personality type and learn how your traits influence your behavior, communication and leadership ability, as well as how to use your skills in the workplace. In my DISC assessment, they pointed out my ability to be a good listener and my effectiveness in relating to others. It is easy for my personality type to focus solely on the needs of others. Learning how to say no became crucial to establishing my work-life balance.

The workplace assessment section gave me tips for self-growth in my work environment. It provided me with the greatest opportunity to reflect. The results forced me to truly look within and find ways to redirect my thinking. One of their tips was to stand up for what I believed in and not be intimidated by strong, extroverted personality types. After reflecting on it for a few days, I decided to work on my boldness during meetings. My personal views needed to be heard, and my first job was to speak up.

By using my voice, I could spark ideas by encouraging different viewpoints and help bring the conversation closer to resolution. Being bold became one of my personal growth activities that year. I even asked my boss to tell me how I was doing and what I could improve on throughout the year. Changing my timid mindset made a big difference. The information from my DISC assessment was beneficial, but things only changed once I evaluated their comments and found ways to apply them to my life. Applying your lessons is critical–do not skip out on reflection. This information helps me understand myself better and allows me to chart my direction toward my North Star. If you have completed a DISC assessment or any other personality assessment before (*Myers–Briggs Type Indicator*, for example), access your results and re-discover the findings.

Another learning experience to consider is asking your spouse, kids, or even your colleagues to take the DISC assessment test. Understanding each person's communication style can improve your connection with them. My husband, based on his personality style, likes direct, to-the-point conversations and short phone calls, while my style is more detail-oriented. Understanding our different communication styles helped me adapt my conversation style to be direct with him over the phone. Instead of telling him about all the great scenes I saw on my way to work, I call him to let him know I made it to work and save the details of the drive for our dinner conversation. This works much better for both of us. I don't feel frustrated that he is not listening, and he resumes what he was doing. Notice that reflecting on our communication preferences created a better situation.

The next step is to find your specific strengths. My favorite assessment is the test from Gallup, which you can also access in the book *StrengthsFinder 2.0* by Tom Rath. This test helps you determine your top five strengths out of the thirty-four most common talents. If you have not taken this test before, I suggest you do. I got the most value by paying for the full report that ranked all thirty-four talents. Your top ten strengths are analyzed, and the test highlights how to maximize your potential and find your blind spots. My biggest takeaway from this book was the potential for people to overuse their strengths. For instance, my number one strength is *woo*. What does that mean? It means my favorite thing is meeting new people. Many are fascinated by my ability to start a conversation in an elevator with a stranger. Since I love meeting people, some perceive me as shallow, like I'm going from one person to another. That would be an example of overusing my strength. Knowing this helps me reflect, assess, and identify a potential area to improve upon.

At my current company, everyone was given the opportunity to do this assessment. It was very impactful. Understanding each other's strengths fostered better collaboration. You can use each other's strengths to foster a great team environment where everyone is encouraged to contribute their best attributes. Managers can use this test to assign work according to their employees' strengths for a win-win situation.

The last step is discovering your internal forces through others. By asking your spouse, kids, parents, siblings, friends, and colleagues for their perspectives, you gain valuable insights. We tend to assess ourselves by our intentions, while others assess us by our actions. Their observations might give you useful insights into your internal forces. Most companies ask for feedback from their employees. Make sure you take advantage of that option; if your company does not offer it, set up a face-to-face session with your colleagues. I do not like the word *feedback* because it sounds like I will receive negative comments. I am afraid they will only highlight my faults. But if I use the word *advice*, it sounds like my colleagues are leaning in to guide me with their words of wisdom to help me succeed. It is a small shift, but it helps me accept their observations about my work.

The purpose of scanning your internal force is to focus on what you do well. It is a morale boost. It best describes who you are at that current moment. Knowing where you stand now will help you discover the direction of your growth journey. If you are ready to take the next step, use the blank section at the end of this chapter to start listing your strengths.

SCAN #2: SCAN YOUR INTERNAL DIALOGUE

Listening to my internal dialogue helps me discover more about myself. I am listening to three distinct types of internal dialogue:

1. Limiting stories

2. Misreading stories

3. Motivating stories

Each story offers important insights into how we process events around us and extract the best strategies for our personal growth. The more you listen to your internal dialogue, the easier it becomes to identify your triggers. Once these triggers are identified and understood, a plan can be created to optimize your future growth.

The first type of story is a limiting story. Limiting stories are negative thoughts we have about ourselves. They can pop up at any time. Pay attention if you hear yourself saying things like, *I can't do this, I don't get it,* or *I suck at this.* These negative thoughts limit our potential to reach our best selves. If you do not see yourself in a positive light, who will? Staying positive does not guarantee success, but it is essential for your growth attitude.

In my son's first-grade class, the teacher would often ask the students if they had an "I can-do attitude." I do not know if my son knew its meaning at the time, but he told me that she was the best teacher he ever had. As a parent, I wish every teacher could get the best out of my son. This teacher made sure to bring a positive attitude to the classroom to activate his interest in learning. Turning negative thoughts into positive ones is a great way to adjust your attitude and grow. Go ahead, turn *I can't do this* into *I can do this*; *I don't get it* into *I will understand it*; *I suck at this* into *I am practicing to get better at this*.

Let me give you another example. My husband is a wonderful cook. It's a great perk! After observing him multiple times during his morning omelet routine, I decided to try it out. The first ten times I made an omelet, there was something wrong with the way it looked. The consistency would be wrong—the ratio of egg and liquid was not right. Or the cooking was off—I burnt several omelets. I almost gave up. However, I noticed something during my attempts. My internal voice was screaming out the entire time, *You can't do this, Marie*. No wonder I felt stressed while I was cooking. How often had I been saying that phrase, and when? It turns out that it's the most common comment I tell myself in any new situation, even at work. I looked back at my personality style and realized I feel uncomfortable when I do something new or outside my comfort zone.

Now everything made sense. I just needed to adjust my attitude. By switching my internal dialogue and using my strengths, I could push through new tasks. With this trigger identified, I can be on the lookout for this phrase whenever trying something new. I can now address this trigger with the attitude that *practice makes perfect* and apply my new phrase, *I am practicing to get better.* This mindset helps me push through, increasing my self-confidence. The environment you are in has no limit. Only you can put a limit on yourself. Ask yourself what limits you from moving forward and what propels you to keep going. Here are four ways to address your limiting stories:

1. Listen to your internal voice

2. Identify the saying that is holding you back

3. Find what drives that saying

4. Replace the saying with something positive

The second type of dialogue, misreading stories, normally includes conversations or interactions with someone else. In this case, while listening and observing, we create a perception from our own experiences that can produce a misleading interpretation of the discussion or situation.

Let's start with an example. In this scenario, I am teaching a Continuous Improvement class. This is a conversation in the class versus a conversation in my head:

Me: "The CEO of our company is very excited about the implementation of Continuous Improvement methodologies."

My head: One of the students just rolled their eyes.

Me: "This is a change in mindset, and only you can enable it."

My head: The same student rolled their eyes.

Me: "Does this statement resonate with everyone?"

My head: For the third time, the student rolled their eyes. They are not engaged; it's disruptive, and I need to address their behavior at the break.

Me: During the break, "I noticed you rolled your eyes at least three times in class this morning. I feel like I am not engaging you with the topic. What can I do better?"

Student: "Sorry about that, I am testing new contact lenses today, and they make my eyes so dry. I found it helps to roll my eyes. I enjoy the class very much!"

My head: Oops!!

How did I come up with such a story? I believed that *rolling your eyes* meant someone was skeptical, not engaged, or bored. I connected this moment to other people over the years who rolled their eyes at my comments. Then I assumed that this student had the same attitude as those people. We all have biases, and one of the most important lessons to take away from this story is to validate my belief. How often do you validate your internal story? Most people find it hard to have those difficult conversations.

Let me give you another scenario. At work, I often mentor people. This is the dialogue I had with one of my mentees who called me in a state of panic:

Mentee: "I will not be able to finish my project. I am leaving the company."

Me: "Oh no, I am sorry to hear that. You found something better?"

Mentee: "Not yet, but I think I am losing my job because of my Continuous Improvement project."

Me: "What? What makes you say that?"

Mentee: "My manager does not like the work I do."

Me: "What makes you say that?"

Mentee: "At our staff meeting, while I was giving an update on the project, the manager gave me a stern look. I am not doing the project as expected, and I am next on the chopping block."

Me: "Did your manager say that directly to you?"

Mentee: "Well, no, the manager does not need to. I can read body language. My manager also canceled our one-on-one for the following day. It's official!"

After probing and verifying with the manager, I learned their brother-in-law got in a car accident. They were preoccupied with other thoughts and not paying attention to the discussion in the staff meeting. The one-on-one meeting was canceled due to a last-minute trip to help their family. My mentee's internal story was not true.

Have you ever experienced something like this? We take our experiences and beliefs into consideration when we interact with others—that is the way it goes. Here are some of the strategies used to prove or disprove my own stories:

+ Stay as neutral and non-emotional as possible. Taking deep breaths helps me stay in a rational state of mind.

+ Always assume good intent.

+ Ask questions to clarify your story. You are searching for clues like a detective.

+ Validate directly with the person. Starting the conversation with "It is my belief" has worked well for me.

I will admit that it is much more difficult for me when my emotions get in the way. Normally this happens more at home than at work. To be transparent, when I am emotional, my internal voice can have both limiting and misreading stories at the same time. I know my emotions are high if I speak the words *always* or *never* internally or externally. For example, if I am tired of doing the dishes, I may get mad at my husband for not helping. I may hear my internal voice say, *He never does the dishes. When I sigh loudly, he should know I need help.* At the time, I may forget that he helped me six of the last ten times I asked, and I also may forget that when we have the TV on, he can't hear me. I reflected on my internal voice, heard myself, and started laughing. *Wow! Am I expecting him to read my mind?* Understanding his personality style and analyzing my misreading story helped me snap out of it. It takes a lot of work to validate your story, but it is essential. If this is an area you would like to improve on, I recommend the book *Crucial Conversations*. It has great tips on mastering dialogue with others.

The third and last dialogue to listen to is your motivating stories. These are the positive dialogues you have with yourself. If you remove all limiting stories, these should be the stories you listen to every day. Motivating stories are what you reach for in times of stress, when you feel down, or sense negative emotions coming on. To spot these negative emotions, you need to constantly listen and look for signs in your self-talk. The key here is to stay positive. Here are the steps I take to keep my positive energy grounded:

1. Repeat my positive *saying* in my head.

2. Write it down to stay focused.

3. Start my morning with the right mindset.

4. If my attitude changes, adjust for the next time and move on.

I will be honest; it takes a lot of energy to change your attitude. It will be a lifelong struggle. Daily practice will make it easier in the long run, and this introspection is essential when seeking your North Star. Some personality types may reach their goals faster, but everyone should be listening to their internal dialogue to learn more about themselves.

SCAN #3: SCAN YOUR REACTIONS

In the last section, we talked about what we say internally and its impact on our best selves. Our inner dialogue produces emotions that the outside world sees via our reactions. The process of turning those thoughts into actions is a great growth opportunity in our quests to become better versions of ourselves. When I think about my reactions, I realize that they are influenced by how stressed, mad, sad, or happy I am. External events also influence our reactions. Understanding our emotional responses to these triggers can help us reach our North Stars.

Let's do a simple game. You are on the road during rush hour, and everyone is trying to get home. Suddenly, someone cuts in front of you with no blinker. What is your first reaction? Be sincere here—your first reaction! *You [explicit],* may come out of your mouth. Most people, at a minimum, would sigh at the violation of their perceived road space. Now imagine the same scenario, but this time the person cutting you off is your wife, coworker, or friend. Are you automatically more patient? I would be. No words were exchanged, just an action seen and perceived as offensive. Our emotional reaction are based on our internal perspectives. Why do we react that way? Commuters have as much of a right to be on the road as you or me. Was the person cutting me off really targeting me on purpose? No, it was not personal.

The amygdala is behind our reactions. The amygdala is an almond-shaped mass in our brains responsible for emotions, survival instincts, and memory. It controls our *fight* or *flight* response. Every piece of information we process goes through the emotional section of the brain before going through the rational part. It is how we are wired. Some people might not even recall what they did during a fight or flight episode. You do not want this to happen to you.

How might we deal with emotional reactions? Here are four steps I have taken that have helped me deal with my reactions:

1. Figure out your physical reactions. My jaw tightens and my heart rate increases when I am getting irritated. If I know that, I can monitor it and confront it with a plan.

2. Find a solution. Taking a deep breath always helps me. Experts agree that this technique reduces the amygdala's fight or flight response.

3. Find a way to redirect your emotions. For fight or flight responses, I keep the big picture in mind or restate the goal of the interaction. When I interact with someone,

I ask questions to calm down. My favorite question is, "Can you tell me more about your point of view?" It gives me time to take a deep breath and seek to understand the other person's point of view.

4. Use a calm voice. My voice will rise when I get emotional. By calming my voice, I de-escalate my emotional response.

Even with all these techniques, a *fight* reaction can happen faster than we think. At my current job, I mentor talented individuals who will be coaching Continuous Improvement projects. The on-the-job training involves sharing my project workload with them. We are in multiple meetings together every day. One day, I personally negotiated to be the only one mentoring a new project. After multiple months of sharing my projects with two mentees, I felt eager to coach by myself. I went to our kick-off meeting; to my surprise, one of my mentees was already in the room. He thought that he would be the mentor for the project. My amygdala went into fight mode. I said, "I cannot get away from you, can I?" Then I thought, *Oh, my gosh! Did I just say that?* As soon as it came out, I regretted it. I immediately said, "I am so sorry. I should not have said that. Let's talk after the meeting in private." After the meeting, we had a really nice discussion. I explained the reasons behind my outburst, and we decided that I should keep this project for myself. The mentee told me that they were not insulted by my comment. That made me feel better. I believe they were sincere.

It happened so fast! A few seconds. In this case, I had to do damage control. I could not get ahead of it. Being vulnerable by showing my emotions and saying sorry was the right thing to do. I love friendly environments and I am people-oriented; this solution to my outburst was the right one for my personality style. You need to find and try strategies that work for you. It starts by watching your reactions and finding a better way to predict them.

Sometimes, learning about your reactions comes from an outside observer. We all have blind spots, and one way to improve your reactions is to ask a friend, spouse, or close colleague to observe you. I call them my *spotters*. They help me understand my shortcomings.

Once, a colleague told me that my non-verbal cue was not *giving grace* to another colleague. He observed that when this person spoke up, I always rolled my eyes at other colleagues. At first, I was surprised. I had no recollection of doing that. But after paying closer attention to myself, I realized he was right. This was another insight into how I could improve myself.

By learning how we react to criticism, we discover how to become our best selves. For example, I once facilitated a staff meeting where a director complained that the agenda items were not well prioritized. Since we ran out of time that day, the director felt my prioritization caused a critical discussion to be postponed.

My boss stepped in and said to the group, "Marie validated the agenda at the beginning of the meeting. What might we do to readjust the agenda from the start?" He turned the mirror on the group to deflect the blame from an individual person, asking a process-based question instead. Team members said it was their job to highlight issues before or at the beginning of the call. At the time, I did not challenge the team, and I gave them a way out of their responsibilities. This experience showed me how to reframe my response to criticism and helped me address similar situations over the years. This example is specific to my personality type, and we all react differently. But how would you react? Is reacting to criticism an area you need to improve?

We have discussed multiple ways to learn from a negative emotional reaction, whether it was from a personal event or an observation by someone else. Understanding how to foster positive reactions is just as important. To reach the best versions of ourselves and continue our journeys, we need to feed on positive energy. How do you react when you are happy?

I show my happiness through my smile. Smiling has always come naturally to me. It was my trademark when I worked at Dunkin' Donuts during college. The simple act of smiling gives me energy. Even on my bad days, I immediately get in a good mood if I see someone smiling at me. It is contagious, free, and easily changes someone's mood. Even on the phone, you can tell if someone is happy if they are smiling as they speak.

Here are some tricks I have used over the years to keep my happy mood:

1. Look into a mirror and practice your smile. This is one routine I do every morning. It helps me wake up, and it gives me confidence for the day. No matter how the day goes, it started well and in a positive light. I even bought a mirror sticker for my son to prompt him to practice every day. I believe it helps. Try it!

2. Notice when you smile. Once while watching *Wheel of Fortune*, my son asked why I was smiling. The contestant had just won, and they were happy, so I felt happy. I never really paid attention to when I was smiling, but I think it is a good mood indicator.

3. Power pose. When I want to boost my self-confidence, I spend one minute with my hands on my waist, smiling and taking deep breaths. This keeps my energy positive. That is the beauty of this small trick: it is a simple action that can be done anytime and anywhere.

These are my methods for keeping high levels of positive energy. Each of us has a different approach to positivity. What is yours?

As you aim for your North Star, you will push yourself into new territories. Observing, understanding, and channeling your reactions increase your self-awareness. Being aware, in turn, makes us see better versions of ourselves.

SCAN #4: SCAN YOUR EXCUSES

In the search to know ourselves, we learn how to discover our strengths and observe our reactions. And as we listen to our internal dialogues, one critical thought affects our progress: excuses. To be honest, I can think of multiple ways I excuse myself from hard tasks. Do not be a procrastinator-in-chief! This is when you need to carefully listen to your internal voice. My one self-improvement goal that I make the most excuses for is my desire to lose weight. I want to lose weight, but coming up with excuses is much easier than doing the work. Who is in control here: me or my brain? I quickly realized that if I don't learn from my excuses, I may not reach my weight loss goal. Let me take you through my three-step discovery process for excuses:

1. Listen to my internal voice and list my excuses

2. Categorize my excuses

3. Develop a strategy for overcoming my excuses

In the first step, listen to your internal voice and list your excuses. Confronting your excuses and finding what drives them is one way to overcome these *speed saboteurs*. After listening to my excuses for a few days, I heard:

- ✦ *I have no time right now to exercise and catch up on work.*

- ✦ *I can exercise next week when I am scheduled to work from home.*

- ✦ *I can lose my extra weight in no time, so I can wait until tomorrow.*

- ✦ *I deserve a food reward for all the work I do.*

Categorizing our excuses offers greater insights into the reasons we fabricate them. My top three excuses can be categorized as a decision story, a belief, or a trigger. Let me explain.

A decision story is when our brains create options to streamline our decisions. Most of the time, these options are fewer and resemble similar experiences and actions taken in the past. The first type of decision story I use involves a choice paradox, or an either-or statement. You can hear this in my first excuse—my only two options are exercising or catching up on work. It is either focusing on my health or my career. My brain pushes for a choice and does not account for a future when I can do both activities on the same day.

The second type of decision story I create is an *if-then* statement. My second excuse is a good example of one. If I start working from home, then I will do my exercise routine. For instance, despite working full-time from home due to the COVID-19 pandemic, it had been more than ten weeks since I had completed an exercise routine. My brain created a decision based on a scenario I had no desire to implement.

After our decision stories come our beliefs, and our beliefs are formed by our past experiences and sometimes our wishful thinking. I clearly remember telling myself the third excuse. *Losing weight always came easy to me. I can lose weight whenever I want.* Notice the word *always* and *whenever*. This statement was true when I was in my 20s or 30s. My brain believes I can do the same thing now. But it is too much work to remember all the other times my weight goal was not met. It is much easier to see experiences as effortless than to see ones that are true to reality. Your beliefs drive your behaviors; if I continue to believe this statement, my attitude toward losing weight will not change. Effortless is not possible anymore.

The last category after beliefs is triggers. In high school, I would reward myself with food when I finished my homework. Ever since then, this habit is so strong that I have driven to the store at 9:30 p.m. to get my fix of high-calorie food. This is what I call a trigger. I have been doing this behavior for so long that rewarding myself with food after a hard day at the office is still a daily struggle. Everyone has triggers. A good friend of mine always smoked after dinner. Thirty years after quitting, he still has the urge. Identifying our excuses helps us discover our limiting stories.

Once you list and categorize your excuses, the last step is to create a strategy to mitigate your limiting stories. A table showing all your observations works well. Here is my strategy for mitigating my weight loss excuses:

	EXCUSES	TYPE OF EXCUSES	LIMITING STORIES	MITIGATION	STRATEGY
1	I have no time right now to exercise and catch up on work	Decision Story (Either or Statement)	See only two choices	Find ways to both exercise and catch up with work	On busy days, find exercises that I can do while working
2	I can exercise next week when I work from home	Decision Story (If-Then Statement)	One condition needs to be met	Don't wait, expand on potential exercise opportunities	Play Pokémon Go; Plan a walking meeting; Take an after-dinner walk; Sing and dance to two favorite songs
3	I lose weight easily, so I can wait to start tomorrow	Belief	Past experience	Validate with facts; Set realistic targets; Change mindset	New mindset: Eating right is a life choice, and I should do everything I can for my health
4	I deserve a food reward for all the work I did	Trigger	High-calorie food reward chosen	Reward with healthy food option that you like	Reward with carrots, or fruits with a little bit of whipped cream

Table 1: Strategy to mitigate my excuses for losing weight.

In Table 1, limiting stories are derived from the type of excuses you tell yourself. The mitigation then shifts your limiting stories, allowing a new strategy to emerge. If you always do what you always did, you will always get the same answer. Use this template to write and analyze your excuses. You may even find different types of excuses and limiting stories. That is fine. Studying your excuses is another important part of understanding your sky.

Since *lack of time* is the most-used excuse, let's go deeper into some tactics we can use to mitigate it. Where are we spending our time? What can we stop doing to give us an extra thirty minutes each day? My optimal time for self-reflection is in the morning. I don't mind getting up at 5:30 a.m. and dedicating thirty minutes to writing or exercising before work. That is my strategy. What time of day works best for you? How can you take advantage of that time and dedicate it to your personal growth? Another trick is to intentionally use the traditional TV time between 8 p.m. and 10 p.m. to work on activities. Since nights are not my optimal time of day, I identify activities that require less brainpower. Watching *TED Talks* on my couch makes me happy; listening to a podcast in the car is another great use of time. Find your own strategies to deal with extra time, then write them down and try a few to discover which ones work best.

We are at the end of phase one–scan your sky. This phase unlocked our potential. It identified our strength zones, changed our internal dialogue into a motivational voice, channeled the energy of our emotions, and confronted our excuses. We now have multiple tools and tips to prevent limitations to our growth. This scan will occur many times throughout your life. As we climb toward our best selves, we will gradually grow, gain new internal forces, create new internal dialogues, face new reactions, and form new excuses. By continuously listening to our stories, we keep our attitudes fixed on our North Stars.

TEST YOUR POINT OF VIEW

Throughout my 30s, I decided to reach for my potential and take the first step toward my best self, my North Star. When destiny pushed me out of my first job, my professional comfort zone, I thought my personal growth would take off because of that decision. Guess what? I was wrong. I never anticipated that my perspective, internal fears, personal approach to growth, and learning model would be repeatedly tested. This prompted me to reconsider my attitude, which has been critical to reaching my growth goal. By working on my point of view and attitude, I could maximize my results.

One of the first lessons of my growth journey was the importance of embracing my point of view. For instance, my core belief of treating everyone with respect was challenged at one of my jobs. Giving everyone an equal chance to make a difference and respectfully empowering employees was essential to a thriving company, but upper management did not share that belief. Our plant manager believed in managers making decisions and union employees executing. I could not manage my employees that way. It was a fight I was willing to make, and I would not back down. Protect the way you think when you know it is right. Even if upper management had their way, I would not have changed anything since I was charting my path.

This experience forced me to fight my fears as well. It made me realize that pushing past my comfort zone, changing my mindset, and learning from my mistakes was the best way to reach my North Star. By testing your perspective, you hit key growth milestones. That is why the next four sections will go deeper into how you can reshape and adapt your point of view. To streamline your growth journey, you need to continuously think about your point of view. This is achieved when you do the following:

1. Chart your point of view

2. Blast your fears

3. Push past your comfort zone

4. Learn from your mistakes

Remember that this is a journey, not an end goal. Throughout your life, you will discover and uncover your potential as you strive for your North Star.

POV #1: CHART YOUR POINT OF VIEW

Every Thursday night, my college faculty would host a party. My friends and I tried to attend as often as possible. Since I was the only one with a car, I would pick up my friends for the party. That way, we did not have to wait for a city bus when we were tired after the party. Since I was the designated driver, I planned to have one beer once I got to the party, dance it off, and stick to water the rest of the night. I felt very proud of this plan. I was responsible and did not endanger my friends. I believed it showed our close friendship.

One year after graduation, we got back together to see how we were all doing. They told me I was not fun in the past since I never drank with them. It surprised me. I quickly quipped that nothing happened to them because I was sober and driving them to their doors at three in the morning. They did not seem to appreciate that fact; they felt that having fun and creating memories with each other was more important. To this day, I feel good about my decision to be different and follow my instinct. If I knew their feelings at the time, I probably would have pushed for us to take the bus. I do not know if they have changed their perspectives all these years later.

We all bring different points of view to the table. In the previous example, I charted and embraced my points of view, and it was liberating. Our unique points of view have been carved from our life experiences, strengths, and personality styles. Your point of view makes you, you. All the personality tests I ever did told me that one percent of the population was like me. I can attest to that for sure. I do feel unique every day, and I love it.

Here are three methods I have used to learn and chart my point of view. This may help you embrace your uniqueness:

1. Choose and chart your strategy

2. Adapt your point of view to new information

3. Keep your expectations grounded as you share your point of view with others

Choose and chart your strategy by considering your beliefs and your life experiences. Let me explain with an example. When I was in 7th grade, my teacher would leave the class door locked in the morning. If we got to school early, we would wait outside in the corridor. One classmate wanted to be the first in the classroom every day. At first, I did not think much of it, but on three occasions, he physically pushed me out of the way just to get closer to the handle of the door. Now I was getting a little bit irate about it. One morning, he pushed his school bag into my rib cage, and I lost it. I lost it so quickly that I do not remember what happened next. But when I came to my senses, I was holding the boy by his shirt against the lockers. I could not believe it. I can be mean, but that is not how I want to be remembered. Even though my classmates applauded afterward, I was not celebrating. At that moment, I decided to manage my temper better and find ways to de-escalate myself. Getting angry was not worth the risk of hurting someone. My emotional reaction to events has dramatically changed since then.

This experience did not represent what I believed or the image I had of my best self. I wanted to be nice and respectful to others. I started to analyze the thought process that led to my outburst. I noticed a level of annoyance with the boy's behavior before my boiling point, which led to my irrational response. I needed to acknowledge these preliminary emotions and develop a strategy that would work for me.

Over the years, I experimented and modified my point of view to mitigate my emotional response. Some worked better than others, but the point here is to try and create a path forward to keep you true to your beliefs. This is the point of the second method, or how to validate and adapt your point of view to new information. Stay open to the perspectives of others; other points of view could improve your approach or process.

They could highlight one of your blind spots, allowing you to improve. All you need to do is listen, be curious, ask questions, and adapt your strategy.

A friend told me that the boy I had slammed into the lockers had a form of autism. This was the first time I had heard about autism. My friend helped me link my classmate's behavior. Now, it made sense to me. If I had shared my frustration with my friend before that day, I would have changed my reaction. Each experience offers new information to chart a new path forward, and you progress over time with all these different points of view. You constantly re-adjust to new information, and you may decide to modify your perspective after listening to someone's rationale. That is fine. Did you truly place yourself in their shoes? I may agree on some components of their view, but on some other aspects, I do not. This is when you hear, "We will just agree to disagree."

This brings us to the last method: keeping your expectations grounded while sharing your point of view with others. I decided a long time ago that I shouldn't be ashamed of sharing my point of view. I do not have control over how others feel about my views. When you keep that in mind, you greatly reduce your frustrations. Not everyone is focused on seeing things from another person's perspective, but when you find that person, you should use the moment wisely.

Fortunately, I have found people around me who are willing to share and brainstorm their different ways of thinking. I regularly have conversations with them to widen my views. We agree that our visions of growth include listening to each other and seeking better ways to improve. Interacting with these friends always gives me energy. You can achieve similar results via books, articles, podcasts, and videos. Remember, we grow by seeking out and sharpening the diversity of our thoughts.

A friend of mine leads a brainstorming exercise that illustrates the importance of diverse points of view. When everyone has taken a seat in the meeting room, he asks everyone to find whichever spot gives them the best viewpoint of the activity. Some participants move to the back of the room, some get closer to the whiteboard, and some might stay in their original spots. When he asks each person to explain their decision, they all provide different reasons. The experiment shows that everyone brings their perspective to the table. How often do we consider someone else's viewpoint?

We should challenge our thinking, belief systems, and perspectives if we want to be the best versions of ourselves. Engaging with diverse thoughts and being curious about other points of view is how we accelerate our trajectories toward our North Stars.

POV #2: BLAST YOUR FEARS

Everyone has fears. The real question is how we use our fears to move forward. The fears I am talking about here are the ones that stop us from reaching our potential. Each of us needs to find the trick that helps us blast our fears and reach our North Stars. But to do that, we need to rethink the word *fear*. Instead of fears, some people see questions to be answered or solutions to be found. They use their perspective or point of view as fuel for reaching their end goal.

Let me offer my definition of fear. Fear is an event, hurdle, or feeling that prevents us from moving forward. It can come from our environment, our perceptions, or even our personality types. Revisit the lessons from phase one to navigate the fears of your personality type.

My greatest fear is social rejection. By publishing this book, one potential fear is that people will not like it. How does this fear affect me? If the main reason for writing my book was social recognition, I might focus only on the negative comments or the people who were not impacted by it. One way to reframe my point of view is to shift my attention to those people I impacted. We cannot please everyone, so why expect it? Now, my driving force is linked to my ability to impact others. To maximize this impact, I asked trusted friends and family to read my book before hiring a great editor. By reframing my perspective, I changed my fears into a way forward. Notice that the strategy did not eliminate my fears but rather changed my mindset. Here are four steps to blast your fears:

1. List the fears holding you back

2. Prioritize which fears you need to work on

3. Determine underlying reasons for your fears

4. Reframe your fears and move forward

When you take the first step and list your fears, categorizing what kind of fear it is can lead you to *known for a while* fears and *never had it* fears. For instance, I do not remember having a fear of public speaking before college. When I presented my college thesis, I had an out-of-body experience. What a weird feeling! It was the first time I had felt this way. I was comfortable talking in class, but presenting in front of the committee made a difference. My thesis was based on several months of data from our labs, and when the committee challenged the data, I started to doubt myself. I felt blindsided by the request to defend my data. In the end, my thesis teacher spoke up and helped me get out of that situation. This experience triggered a fear of public speaking. In the following days, I reflected on the incident to extract reasons for my reaction.

My fear was not public speaking but a fear of not being able to answer follow-up questions. Ever since then, my strategy has been to practice my presentations and anticipate potential questions. My perspective was *I need to know the answer*, which put more pressure on me. Once I felt that pressure, I had the out-of-body experience. This is my hypothesis; I am not a doctor. But I believe that the stress of the situation contributed to the episode.

I still had to reframe my point of view to *I may not know all the answers, and that's ok.* Today, if I do not know the answer, I will say, "I did not think about this angle, so I don't have an answer for you at this time," or "I don't know, but I can find out for you." As you can see, your strategy needs to be personalized according to your own analysis and judgment. Reframing is essential to moving forward and blasting your fears. As discussed in phase one, this can be used for your internal voice, and your attitude, or perspective.

How you react to life's unplanned moments makes a big difference. Let me explain with a simple example. When our son was young, my husband and I decided to call all unplanned moments *adventures*. It turned negative situations, such as flat tires or missed flights, into positive situations. Just the word *adventure* makes it fun! It makes me smile. It also affected how our son responded to his own unplanned moments. We intentionally set up a positive environment for all of us. I made this change when I observed the negative impact my bad emotional responses had on our family. Listening to our physical and emotional triggers is a useful way to spot potential fears.

Observe how you react to events and ask your boss or spouse for their insights and observations. Does anything stick out? I have noticed that my first reaction, when I am asked to execute a new task at work, is *Nope, I do not want to do that.* Ever since I reframed my perspective, I stop and ask myself why. The important takeaway here is to evaluate why you are having this reaction. If a path forward is not evident to me within the first few seconds of a task, I do not feel equipped to do it. That is my reaction to fear of the unknown, and it can be enormously influential. By asking close friends how they would approach a similar situation and discussing my strategy with them, I improve my approach and blast my fears.

In this example, my strategy was to evaluate whether or not this new work task would help me in my growth direction. Most of the time, they do. Instead of assuming you should not do this, ask yourself if this is something you were meant to do. Would that change your perspective? We will spend the next two chapters diving into how you can push past your comfort zone and deal with the fear of failure.

POV #3: PUSH PAST YOUR COMFORT ZONE

Leaving your comfort zone is crucial to reaching your North Star. There are two scenarios that allow you to push past your comfort zone: events you react to and events where you seize an opportunity. In both cases, you need to decide to push yourself. To achieve personal growth, you need to reach for newer and higher goals. Your resilience, grit, and attitude will help you get there. Remember, reaching your North Star is a step-by-step process. Here are the steps I discovered to push myself beyond my comfort zone:

1. Practice daily

2. Challenge yourself

3. Seek new experiences

4. Get a mentor

The best way to get better is to practice daily. Remember, practice makes perfect! By practicing daily, you achieve two goals: you move gradually toward your best self by speeding up your improvement, and you keep your intent to change at the front of your mind. I call this daily regiment the vitamins of your personal growth. For example, when I wanted to improve my leadership skills, I read or watched leadership videos every day. During the weekends, when I had more time, I invested in deep-dive learning sessions about leadership. The key here is to be deliberate and focus on a priority you need to improve on. Keeping in mind the reason will help with your motivation. Listen to your internal voice and watch for triggers that may derail your efforts.

This daily practice may challenge the way you are doing things now. How can you practice pushing yourself in your everyday life? Let's say you want to work on your resistance to change. Switching up your morning routine may be a daily practice that is simple and low-risk. As you get comfortable with this new routine, change it up again. I got comfortable with my routine after practicing three times. By challenging yourself daily, you determine your future comfort zone. If you cannot find ways to challenge yourself via existing routines, the internet is full of people attempting their own challenges. My friend loves watching self-help YouTube videos, for instance.

When you practice daily and challenge yourself, it is important to seek new experiences to stay curious. My favorite method is observing colleagues. By watching how they do things, I can ask clarifying questions to understand what is different about their approach. To learn from others, you first need to acknowledge that you can learn from them. I have seen people listening but not engaging; they were more worried about showing off than listening to others or seeking new experiences. Do not waste that opportunity. For instance, one of my colleagues is an ace at analyzing and displaying data. Because I asked him for help, he walked me through his step-by-step analysis and shared his best practices for showcasing findings. He was generous with his time and instrumental in my success with subsequent presentations. Look for new lessons, prioritize the critical skills you need, and implement them into your daily routine. The last step is to find a mentor. Having a mentor helped me stay focused and prioritized on the right skills. I am interested in many skills, so I can wander from my priorities for days if I am not careful. For me, I needed an accountability manager. But first, let me clarify my definition of a mentor, an accountability manager, and a coach.

A mentor is someone who guides you through his or her experiences/expertise. An accountability manager is an activator, someone who encourages you to execute. In some cases, they can be the same person. A coach will ask questions to help you uncover your path and guide you to extract your own answers. If you do get a coach, make sure they have been trained as one. If your coach starts sharing their experiences with you instead of asking questions, they are mentoring you. Being a coach myself, I know how tempting it is.

My coach, David Martin, helped me uncover my desire to write a book. His questions made me realize my preferred medium for reaching more people and my life's purpose. The progress I made with David was the best *aha* moment toward my future goals. Sharing my perspective and efforts with my coach helped me push past my comfort zone. Just talking to him about my week revealed insights into my mindset.

On this point, let me go back to the earlier story where my colleague helped me be more successful. I personally felt he was mentoring me. Debriefing with him highlighted the fact that these new skills were expected of me from the start. Growing my skillset gave me a great feeling of accomplishment, but the long hours were not recognized by my executive director, leaving me disappointed and tired. Pushing outside your comfort zone is the right thing to do, but sometimes your expectations around those efforts need to be adjusted.

With this final example, you can clearly see that the lessons from earlier chapters (like listening to your internal voice) play an important role. The four-step process is a cycle that we will constantly repeat, but it helps us reach our North Stars.

POV #4: LEARN FROM YOUR MISTAKES

One way to confront the fear of failure is to encourage yourself to learn from your mistakes. How do you react when you are failing? For me, the fear of failure became an excuse not to push toward my growth goals. Here are a few tricks I use to shift my mindset:

1. Reframe failing

2. Activate your curiosity

3. Expect mistakes

The purpose of shifting your point of view is to accelerate your learning curve. Reframing *failing* to *experimenting* helped me feel more willing to try new things. By experimenting, you test a new theory or skillset to allow yourself space to learn. And since we are moving toward our North Stars in incremental steps, the only way to go up is to learn our way up. The easiest way to do that is to learn from our mistakes. You want to assume the mindset of failing now to learn faster.

These techniques are much easier to execute when you have no time constraints or external pressures. Fortunately, several of the companies I worked for valued experimentation and failing fast. But even if yours does not, you can activate your curious mindset, the second step. When your experiment fails, perk up, switch your mindset, and learn from the moment. Can you take away anything positive from the situation? Let me explain how my curious mindset was once activated at work.

My boss had asked me to facilitate a root cause analysis session, and I would be leading the discussion with a team of professionals. Before the session, I created an agenda and process to brainstorm with the team. I was well prepared, but we were not even ten minutes into the meeting when I realized that my process was not working for this group. I could not get them to engage with my technique. At this rate, I would not get anything out of the session. Everyone in the room had busy schedules, so rescheduling the meeting was out of the question. It was obvious to me I needed to salvage the meeting. I decided to abandon my prepared agenda and ask questions. From the answers I received, I realized that this group needed to list experienced issues instead. I switched techniques and asked them to write all their issues on Post-It Notes. This helped the team see potential places for improvement and gained their buy-in into the process.

I was flexible, adaptable, and willing to fail fast, which made a difference in this session. The outcome would have been different if I had focused on my original plan and ignored the third and final step. Unexpected events will happen, and you will make mistakes, so learn to expect them. This meeting taught me to go with the flow and have fun with it. The only thing you have control over is how you react to your environment.

What should you do if your business meeting or presentation is not salvageable? Just ask for help! It is OK to be vulnerable and acknowledge the failure of your plan. Here, it is important to remember that you are not a failure. Your plan just needed a different strategy. The first time I taught how to use a statistical tool, the lesson went so poorly that my boss had to come in and teach the module. I was "in training" as a teacher, but it was still hard to fail in front of everyone. What I learned from that experience was priceless and helped me become better, faster.

You can see that your journey will have cycles of growth and lessons. These are the key attitudes you must have to reach your

North Star. Remember that this is a journey, not an end goal. Having the right mindset and attitude keeps your self-growth alive, and it starts with thinking about your views, learning from them, and uncovering new ones.

ACT TO REACH YOUR NORTH STAR

By the time I was out of my 30s, I had reached a point where I could be more intentional about my personal growth. I needed to act and develop a plan now if I wanted to be the best I could be by my 40s. To reach my North Star, I needed to follow three instructions:

1. Determine my destination

2. Set my voyage

3. Start my engine

Determining your next destination allows your journey to fall into place. By setting your end goal, you can map your voyage and make clear how to get there. To illustrate this, let me take you back to my early 40s. I had just landed my first job as a Continuous Improvement manager. A consultant at my last job trained me for this position, but my new boss wanted me to pass the ASQ Certification exam to prove my knowledge. Easy enough, all I had to do was buy a book, study, practice the materials, and pass the four-hour exam. But as I studied for the test, I realized I did not know everything about Continuous Improvement (CI). If my goal was to know all CI techniques, I had a lot of work to do.

Learning new things had always been fun, but being intentional about my learning was a new approach for me. I took a few weeks to analyze my strengths, fears, and what pushing outside my comfort zone would look like. I envisioned what reaching my potential in CI might look like. The vision I had of my best self became my objective for the next decade. At the end of my 40s, I wanted to be the best CI trainer. By identifying my learning gaps, listening to my internal voice, and pushing outside my comfort zone, I determined four main actions that I needed to complete to achieve my goal. I called these actions *voyages* or *stages*:

1. Get my master's degree in business administration (MBA)

2. Learn all CI methodologies

3. Practice teaching those methodologies

4. Mentor multiple candidates

Once the direction of my personal growth became clear, it dawned on me that my current company may not help me reach my goal. To fulfill my vision, I would eventually need to get hired by a multinational company. And to be hired by a bigger company, I would need a master's degree. Finally, by getting an MBA in finance, I would address one of my learning gaps–being comfortable with financial reports. It was a win-win.

At the time, I remember my internal voice saying, *You can't do that! Do you remember how much trouble you had finishing your bachelor's degree? You couldn't focus! Besides, you have a full-time job that requires you to travel to our company's manufacturing plants. How will you get it done? What about your nine-year-old son? Are you willing to give up time with him? And how will you pay for it?* As you can see, my fears were out in force.

Even with all those thoughts, I soldiered through and planned the steps I needed to take to make this goal a reality. I started with my first voyage–getting an MBA. Here is how I planned to get my MBA:

1. Verify if my company has a School Assistance Program

2. Budget MBA costs

3. Search for an MBA school close to me

4. Choose an MBA program that will fit my work schedule

5. Talk to my family about my goal

6. Gather documents and apply to my chosen MBA program

7. Start classes

Once you develop your plan, you need to start it–do not wait! In my case, I discovered a few days after making my plan that my company had a School Assistance Program and that they were willing to pay half of the cost. I also found out that a school near me offered an accelerated online MBA for the first time. This meant I could complete the MBA online in less than eighteen months. Wow, I could not believe it! The online option would take less time away from my family and help with my travel schedule at work.

Even when you feel like you are climbing Mount Everest, take your first step for greater insights and rewards. My journey to my North Star was not easy. I learned and discovered invaluable lessons along the way that made the journey worth it. Action helps you realize your North Star. The beauty of a life devoted to personal growth is that ending one journey makes you want to start another.

ACTION #1: KNOW YOUR DESTINATION

Understanding the destination, the end game, of your personal growth journey is the first step toward your North Star. This step may require you to take a deep dive into yourself if you have not yet defined your North Star. But it is critical to set a goal if you want to reach it quickly and effectively. Your destination is a long-term plan, and to reach it, you will need multiple short-term plans. To unlock your destination, follow these four steps:

1. Analyze who you are

2. Storyboard your destination

3. Create your vision statement

4. Craft your goal

During the first phase of this book, scan your sky, you took the time to explore yourself. Using that information, and by answering a few questions, you can achieve a deeper understanding of yourself, thus focusing on your potential. These questions helped me analyze myself:

+ What are my strengths?

+ What am I passionate about?

+ What is important to me?

+ What makes me happy?

+ What is my purpose?

+ What do I want to leave as my legacy?

I will be transparent here and share my answers to make it easier for you to follow along and see my thought process. Remember, your analysis represents what you know at this point in time. It is your best estimate of who you are and how you feel. To demonstrate, this is my assessment from 2015:

+ What are my strengths?
  - Good listener – loves connecting with others (talking and learning)
  - Teacher – shares CI lessons
  - Positive – smiles a lot
  - Cheerleader – loves encouraging others

+ What am I passionate about?
  - Helping others by teaching and coaching CI
  - CI skills, tools, processes, and personal growth
  - Leadership skills and their application to CI culture
  - Ongoing learning from others

+ What is important to me?
  - My family
  - Work-life balance
  - Helping others

+ What makes me happy?
  - Connecting and sharing with others
  - Making a difference to others – adding value

✦ What is my purpose?

  • Helping others through my strengths

✦ What do I want to leave as my legacy?

  • Added value to the lives of a lot of people

Let's analyze this exercise. All my strengths and my personality profile paint me as an advisor, teacher, and coach to others. I am passionate about CI processes and personal growth. I spend a lot of time learning about leadership. Connecting with others is important to me and makes me happy. For those reasons, I feel my purpose is to help others. I want to leave a legacy where I have added value to the lives of as many people as possible. Now, with all these thoughts together, it helped to create a vision storyboard.

Armed with a pencil and eraser, I drew my destination, my future potential. If you are telling yourself, *I cannot draw*, so did I. But if I am honest, it was a fun part of the process. The analytical side of my brain complemented the artistic side. It made me focus on the big picture of my North Star and helped me clarify my vision. Here is a pictorial representation of my drawing:

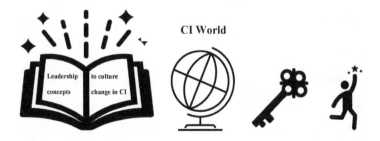

Once I felt good about my storyboard, I shared it with my family and close friends. Present your vision storyboard to at least three people; showing my pictures and explaining my story helped me perfect my vision. With confidence and clarity, you can put your images into words, thus forming your destination vision statement.

Your one-phrase statement should represent your emotions, the driving force you felt as you drew your destination. Here is my destination vision statement from 2015: *Write a book about leadership and culture change concepts to help Continuous Improvement professionals succeed.*

Once you draft your destination vision statement, you need to craft what success would look like. Your goal should also be simple, one or two sentences only. Like with any goal, it needs to be written in a SMART way. My definition of a SMART goal is a goal that is *simple, motivating, achievable, results-based,* and *time-based.* Make it specific enough to motivate you.

Your destination goal can be adjusted over time. Since it is a long-term goal, the closer you get to your destination, the sharper your goal becomes. Here is my destination goal from 2015: *By the end of 2023, my book will add value to at least one million people in the process improvement world.*

To help you work things out, the questions in this chapter are duplicated below. Take your time answering each question and have fun with it—own your journey!

DEFINING YOUR DESTINATION – QUESTIONS TO ANSWER:

What are my strengths?

_____

_____

_____

_____

What am I passionate about?

_____

_____

_____

_____

What is important to me?

_____

_____

_____

_____

What makes me happy?

_____

_____

_____

_____

What is my purpose?

_____

_____

_____

_____

What do I want to leave as my legacy?

_____

_____

_____

_____

Reviewing my answers, what direction do I need to take to reach my potential?

_____

_____

_____

_____

Which drawing represents your destination the most?

_____

_____

What is your destination vision statement?

_____

_____

_____

_____

What is your SMART destination goal?

_____

_____

_____

ACTION #2: SET YOUR VOYAGE

In the last chapter, you discovered your destination or the direction you want your personal growth journey to take. Since your destination is a long-term goal, you need to accomplish your destination in stages. To do that, you will need to define those stages or short-term goals. To set your voyage:

1. Identify the gaps between you and your destination

2. Determine and prioritize your short-term voyages

3. Set dates for your voyages

If you want to reach your North Star, the first step is to identify any existing gaps. What is missing that is preventing you from accomplishing your vision? Put some time aside to go back to your destination statement and destination goal. Collect your thoughts to close the loop. It helps me to write it down. If you remember from our last chapter, my destination statement was: *Write a book about leadership and culture change concepts to help Continuous Improvement professionals.* My destination goal was: *By the end of 2023, my book will add value to at least one million people in the process improvement world.*

To add value to the CI world, I needed to pull from my work experience. In 2015, however, the position I had was not in CI. This was my first obvious gap; I needed to go back to CI. My new role needed to give me experience with leadership concepts around culture change, since most of these strategies are implemented at the start of a new CI deployment. To reach my goal, the new CI company would need to be at a starting-level CI implementation.

My second gap was a book. I did not have a published book in my name. The driving force behind why I wanted to publish a book was the lack of books about leadership in CI. When you are hired as an expert in CI, you are asked to influence others and motivate them to improve their processes. Most of the time, the people you are helping do not report to you. To increase their level of success and the organization's, your soft skills need to be used daily. Those skills are not explained in any book or class. I have been looking for these insights all my career.

The last gap was adding value to one million people. Could I achieve this goal with a book? Possibly, but very unlikely. Where would I get the reach necessary to accomplish it? I could work for a big Wall Street company, but selling your book is a conflict of interest. Reaching those types of companies requires me to start my own consulting business.

With those three gaps identified, I had my three stages or voyages. Prioritizing was easy since each stage depended on the other, essentially building on each other. Here are my stages or voyages spelled out:

1. Find a job in process improvement

2. Publish a book on the leadership concepts of Continuous Improvement

3. Transition from a corporate job to my own consulting firm

After determining and prioritizing your short-term goals, your last task is to calculate the completion dates of your voyages. At this stage, these dates are rough estimates. By starting with your end date, you force yourself to plan according to your long-term goals and North Star. For instance, I needed to reach my destination by the end of 2023. Working backward from that date, how much time would it take me to add value to at least one million people after starting my consulting firm? The answer might be measuring it via the number of followers on my company's Facebook account. My high-level estimate in 2015 was one year. Therefore, making the transition from a corporate job to owning my own consulting firm needed to be completed by the end of January 2023.

I could apply this method to other short-term goals as well. Creating enthusiasm for my new book and generating enough leads to leave my corporate job would take a minimum of one year. Therefore, I would need to publish my book by the end of January 2022. To write and edit my book in a part-time capacity should take an additional two years. Finally, practicing leadership concepts on a CI deployment would take another two years. With all that information, I had to find a job in CI by the end of January 2017. When I calculated all these dates, it was August 2015; I estimated a minimum of one year to find the right CI deployment, so I needed to start as soon as possible. Having dates helped me figure out if I was ahead or behind my plan. Here is what my dates look like in a table:

#	Voyage Description	Target Completion Date
1	Find a job in process improvement	January 31st, 2017
2	Publish a book on the "leadership concepts of Continuous Improvement"	January 31st, 2022
3	Make the transition from a corporate job to owning my own consulting firm	January 31st, 2023

In Appendix 1, you can see my final documented destinations. Use the questions below to establish your gaps, voyages, and destinations.

SET YOUR VOYAGE – QUESTIONS TO ANSWER:

What are the current gaps between you and your destination?

_____

_____

_____

What are your short-term goals or voyages?

_____

_____

_____

_____

What are the completion dates for each of your short-term goals?

#	Voyage Description	Target Completion Date
1		
2		
3		

ACTION #3: START YOUR ENGINE

In the last chapter, you learned how to plan your short-term goals or voyages. That plan is half the battle. You still need to learn how those voyages get you to your targeted date. To start your engine and reach your North Star, follow these clear, attainable, and time-bound steps:

1. Restate your goals and timeline

2. Identify gaps between you and your goals

3. Determine what actions help you accomplish your voyage

4. 3, 2, 1, liftoff!

In this chapter, you need to get into what activities help you complete each voyage. Start by restating one of the voyages and its timeline, as discussed in the last chapter. Let us take my third voyage as an example: *Starting my own business.* By January 31st, 2023, I will transition from a corporate job to my own consulting firm. Identifying the gaps was easy. I found four main activities that I needed to accomplish:

1. Business plan activities – To be completed by the end of 2015

2. Personal growth activities – To be completed after the business plan

3. Promotion, networking, and marketing activities – To be completed by July 2022

4. Business material activities – To be completed by the end of 2022

Your timeline needs to match your voyage deadline. If I need to start my business by January 31st, 2023, my materials, marketing, and readiness need to be prepped by the end of 2022. Notice that this is your best estimate at the time for your long-term plan. Remember that some unknowns might still need to be ironed out. That is fine. You are still developing your plan; it is a working document. Do not wait too long to complete your vision.

Looking back at my example, you may notice that my personal growth activities depended on my business plan. Sometimes, you just do not know which direction to take. When this happens, finding clarification in another activity might be the right thing to do. In my case, I invested time early on to determine my high-level business plan and realized an important detail in my vision. My book would help me reach my destination goal of one million people, but the royalties associated with a book would not be enough to fund my company. I needed to think of other ways to increase my revenue. After asking some of my friends in similar situations, I decided to supplement my income through corporate clients, speaking engagements, workshops, and coaching. This plan then helped me determine the specifics of my personal growth activities and deadlines.

✦ Personal growth activities – Completed by the end of 2020

- Improve speaking skills – End of 2018

- Improve coaching skills – End of 2019

- Improve selling skills – End of 2020

I divided my growth goals across three years. You can also add more details under each goal if you prefer. This might be necessary if you have a big destination. Try your best to plan your first voyage and put down your best time estimate. The last chapter will explain any activities or time adjustments needed along your journey.

The process explained in the last two chapters can work for big or small goals. I used the same process to lose weight as I did to plan for buying a new house. Try it on a smaller goal first if you feel unsure. The critical point of this chapter is to follow your plan. For me, this is the hardest part. Per my personality type, I love to plan. I can easily get stuck reflecting and making new action plans but not following through. Knowing this helps me push myself at the right moment. Another way to keep the pressure on is to team up with someone who can be your accountability manager. My son is mine. A friend or mentor can also help you stay on track.

Similarly, another way to create energy around your plan is to tell other people about your project. You are more likely to act on it when you tell people. When I started to write my book, I told many of my coworkers and noticed it helped me feel motivated. I figured this would push me to do it faster, and it did at first. What it did not prepare me for was how much time it would take to complete. Now, when my colleagues ask how my book is coming along, I must be vulnerable and honest. It is hard to admit when you are falling behind on your timeline. But even in failure, you can add value to others. In the past year, multiple people have told me how meaningful and impactful my vulnerability around this failure was to them.

To increase the odds of your success and get the most bang for your buck, make your plan a part of your daily habits. Your success and growth are linked to your day-to-day focus. If your goal is to change a behavior, for instance, every day repetition will speed up your growth. For me, I am a better writer if I practice day after day. You are creating a habit; that is the key word here, habit.

Continue to apply your learnings from the first two phases of this book. Listen to your internal voice for excuses and negative dialogue. Keep your point of view clear by blasting through your fears, creating excitement outside your comfort zones, and learning from your mistakes. Remember, it is a journey.

Reflecting on when I experienced exponential growth, I noticed one other characteristic of my success. I felt a stronger desire to act and take charge of my growth during those times. Basically, I realized your success is proportional to your belief that growth will not automatically happen. Get outside your comfort zone, challenge yourself, experience new things, and hone your point of view.

Remember that getting outside your comfort zone is a decision. It is a willingness to move forward with a mindset to experiment and learn. For example, my initial Continuous Improvement training course was four weeks long and had four people from the same office participating. For the first three weeks of classes and dinners, I spent time with my colleagues. By the last week of training, I realized I was not connecting with the classmates who were not my colleagues. In that last week, I pushed myself out of my comfort zone and interacted with new people every day. I am still friends with the classmates I met that week. I learned so much about them, from how they were solving issues at work to personal hobbies. I even parasailed with one classmate that week—the only time in my life, too. Pushing through your fears, breaking the status quo, creating a new path forward—this is how you find rewarding experiences. Action leads to growth!

To help you start your engine, use Appendix 2 and the template on the book's website. We are at the end of phase three, and you now have all the tools you need to determine your destination, voyages, and action plans for your journey to your North Star. Congratulations! Enjoy liftoff to your best self!

SET YOUR VOYAGE –
QUESTIONS TO ANSWER:

What are the goals and timelines of your voyages?

_____

_____

_____

_____

What are the current gaps between you and your voyages?

_____

_____

_____

_____

What are the action items for each voyage?

_____

_____

_____

_____

Liftoff – What thoughts help you feel enthusiastic about your action plan?

_____

_____

_____

_____

REFLECT ON YOUR DESTINATION

I n my mid-40s, I discovered that being intentional with my personal growth needed to include reflections on the lessons I learned during my journey. As you grow, you learn, and those lessons can influence your path. Extracting those lessons becomes essential to evaluating the actions leading to your goal. It is like asking your GPS to warn you if there is traffic ahead, but you ignore it. To increase the chance of reaching your North Star, you need to do the following:

1. Look back at the earth to evaluate your direction and make adjustments

2. Shoot for the stars to feel energized by your journey

Let me explain how to evaluate your direction and make adjustments, which are instrumental skills to your success. This year, one of my goals was to lose my Christmas vacation weight before spring vacation. To achieve my target number, I needed to lose two pounds a week. My action items were to make the right food choices every day, stop snacking in the evening, and walk 10,000 steps per day. Once a week, I would monitor my weight loss. After a few weeks, I saw I hit a plateau; my weight was not changing. In desperation, I emailed my doctor for advice. He answered with two questions, "Are you monitoring your calorie intake? Are you eating less than 2,000 calories a day?"

I remember thinking, *I am not exceeding my daily calorie intake.* To make sure, I started to count my calories for the next few days. He was right! I was taking in too many calories. I had to change to reach my goal. I updated my action item list to include daily monitoring of calorie intake. With that small adjustment, I got closer to my goal.

Reflection increases your chance of success and expands your awareness. It is your way of confirming the right path forward. To persevere in your quest, you need to pay attention to your energy level. Your energy is the fire inside you that fuels your focus and determination. The journey will not always be easy, but these reflection techniques offer help along the way. To give you all the help you need to reach your North Star, we will expand on those techniques in the last two chapters.

REFLECT #1: LOOK BACK AT THE EARTH

Your liftoff was successful, and you are on your way toward your North Star. Look back at the path you took and confirm that this is the correct direction to your destination. Remember, at this stage, the key steps to success are:

1. Debrief and extract lessons learned

2. Adjust plan as needed

The main purpose of debriefing and extracting is to ensure that your action plan is still serving your needs. Every time we grow, we learn. By asking questions about your experiences, you can see if you achieved the expected outcome. You can use the following questions to get started:

1. How did this experience make you feel?

2. What were you expecting?

3. What were your assumptions?

4. What did you learn that you need to change?

For example, in my voyage to publish a book, my first action was to ask what steps I needed to take to write a book. These questions helped me debrief and extract the right information. Here were my answers:

1. How did this experience make you feel? It made me feel overwhelmed with all the information and steps

for publication. It will take me longer than my expected deadline, and I will need help.

2. What were you expecting? That I could find everything I needed to know about publishing in one book. However, I had to expand my research and connect with an author to learn more.

3. What were your assumptions? Easy entry into the field of publishing and a higher book royalty return to the author.

4. What did you learn that you need to change? I had to write two to three chapters of my book before I could submit it to an agent—this would add a step to my action plan. The packet sent to the agent needed to contain a market analysis of similar books—adding another step. I also needed to buy the *Writer's Market* or a listing of book publishers and literary agents with their genres and specialties. I do not have a step for that. Due to these new tasks and the length of the voyage ahead, I learned I needed to be resilient. I asked my mentor to keep me motivated, accountable, and encouraged. I also learned to keep my destination statements in front of me during the journey.

As you can see, a straightforward goal like publishing reaps many benefits from a period of reflection. Reflections are a great way to move forward and produce incremental growth. They should be used to assess and confirm the direction you are taking. They are packed with lessons and experiences that make you change for the better. In some instances, a failure in your plan is good if it prompts a reflection.

As part of my voyage to publish my book, one step was finding an agent. I had a lot of work to do before I could submit my book to an agent, as I had learned. After months of hard work, I was finally ready. Most agents take two months to read your packet and respond. Since they have so many requests, you only get an answer if they choose you. Well, I am still waiting for that answer. I felt rejected and discouraged after investing so much time in my aspiration. With no answer, it's hard to know what was wrong. The only thing I controlled was my ability to reflect on the experience.

I started this reflection internally before engaging with others in my process. Here were some of my answers to *What did you learn that you need to change?*

+ The book felt like a research paper. It did not read like "tricks from Marie" but more like insights from different authors.

+ The topic was very focused on Process Improvement, limiting my potential audience.

✦ The conventional way of publishing a book had changed. Self-publishing, for example, may be a better fit.

With those thoughts in mind, everything became obvious; I needed to pivot and create a new destination vision statement that would feel like my own. In 2019, I changed my statement to the following: *By 2023, I will help one million people reach their full potential—their North Star—through my personal growth concepts.* After making that change, I noticed I had much more energy for the book.

Reflecting guides your next steps and is good for you. But in some instances, reflection comes with its own set of pitfalls. I have been there. One of my strengths is my ability to reflect on my experiences. Yet my biggest pitfall is overusing this strength and not getting to my action plan. I need to be aware of the time I spend reflecting since I love it so much and make sure I incorporate actions into my reflection.

Reflecting is a great way to circle back and align with yourself. You are listening to your internal voice—what is your internal voice telling you? Do you hear fears and excuses, or are you putting yourself down? This is a great way to scan your sky, as discussed in phase one. Did you establish a strategy for that dialogue? If yes, go back and apply that strategy. If not, how might you turn your internal dialogue into a positive one?

Pushing yourself beyond your comfort zone takes daily effort and focus. Remember, it is a journey; you are looking for incremental changes in your behavior! It will feel uncomfortable, and that is a good sign. Learn to embrace the feeling of being uneasy. Be honest with your feelings and learn from your reactions.

In phase four, you are looking for signs that you need to readjust your plan. One visual clue is if your dates are slipping. When I miss my preset deadlines, it is a telling sign that my prioritization needs to be reevaluated. This is totally fine; that is the purpose of reflection. You learn new insights on your journey, and adjustments will be made. Keep listening to your motives as you reflect. Are you using excuses? Do you have the right mindset? I prefer doing the easiest activities first. My dates help me stay focused on the right activities.

Your growth journey is a cycle. You determine your destination, set the voyages, start your engine, reflect, and adjust according to the lessons learned along the way.

LOOK BACK AT THE EARTH – QUESTIONS TO ANSWER:

What did you learn after reflecting?

_____

_____

_____

Do you need to adjust your action items?

_____

_____

What is hindering your progress?

_____

_____

_____

What is your internal voice telling you?

_____

_____

_____

_____

REFLECT #2: SHOOT FOR THE STARS

Shooting for the stars means activating your resilience and sustaining your commitment to your destination. Maintaining your energy level and dedication is essential to reach your North Star. You will have good days and bad days, but these three tricks help me stay focused and push onward:

1. Look at your accomplishments

2. Find energy in your environment

3. Momentum is your friend

Just like driving a car, keep your eyes on the road ahead, but check your rearview mirror from time to time. Looking back at the ground you already covered and the hurdles you surpassed gives you a sense of accomplishment. Imagine climbing a long flight of stairs; each landing gives you a chance to look back and see the number of steps you already took. If you are out of breath or energy, you can rest a little, take a deep breath, and continue your climb. On most of my low days, this technique helps me press on.

Looking back can also reveal your *sunk cost*. A sunk cost is the total amount of time, money, and effort you devoted to reaching your destination. For example, I spent a lot of time and effort working toward my weight goal before spring vacation. Understanding my sunk cost helped me stay on track with my food choices, preventing me from undermining all my efforts. This motivated me to continue eating better to reach my weight loss target.

On the days when this does not work, I find energy in my environment. Your best friend, spouse, mentor, or accountability partner can act as your personal cheerleader. By connecting with them, you help yourself take the next step. Understanding what motivates you and sharing it with your friends and family becomes a fire starter for action. Your motivation arrives in different forms: the challenge itself, the recognition and appreciation of others, or the level of success. Get energy from your cheerleaders and surround yourself with positive and encouraging people to keep your journey alive.

The third and final tip to boost your journey is using momentum as a fuel source. Once you create momentum, moving forward becomes easier. The more your daily activities incorporate productive actions, the more momentum you gain. It speaks to the importance of being intentional in the pursuit and maintenance of your momentum. But do not forget to pay attention to the ways you could be damaging your momentum. When writing gets difficult, I am easily distracted by my surroundings. My trigger is a loss of focus. Taking a deep breath and writing an imperfect thought helps me maintain my momentum. When I fail to bring back my focus, I take a break or do something else. That is fine—sometimes you just need it.

Keep your energy and momentum high, and you will reach your North Star. You now have all the tools and knowledge you need to land!

SHOOTING FOR THE STARS – QUESTIONS TO ANSWER:

What motivates you?

_____

_____

_____

_____

How will you keep your momentum?

_____

_____

_____

What excuses damage your momentum?

_____

_____

_____

_____

What do you tell yourself to negate your excuses?

_____

_____

_____

_____

I Believe You Can Reach Your North Star!

We started this book with an aspiration: *Be the best you can be.* You now have the steps to make it happen. It is all up to you! I believe in you, and I know you can do it. Allow me to be your internal cheerleader, your special rocket booster. You need energy and motivation to continue pushing toward your destination. Identify the sources of energy that are guaranteed to recharge your batteries. A walk on the shore of Lake Huron does wonders for my energy level, for instance.

Persistence and dedication will be your greatest assets to get you through your growth journey. Yet, I have days where those attributes are not enough. When I feel overwhelmed by everything going on around me, that feeling of being out of control, I first need to acknowledge it. Once it has been identified, I stop everything, when possible, to regroup my energy. Isolating myself from everyone and taking long, deep breaths stop me from panicking. Ninety-five percent of the time, I am overwhelmed by the next stage of my plan, not the current one. Looking at the bigger picture and focusing my energy on my current steps help tremendously. Discover your triggers and plan accordingly.

Keep your priorities in front of you to reduce stress and prevent your mind from running wild. Unknowns drive me crazy, and workload is another source of anxiety. As I write this, we are in the process of moving to a new house. I found that regular reminders about why we are moving helps. We visualize our new life in the house, our compass, and repeat the reasons it is worth the effort.

Two final, yet essential, reminders for your growth journey: keep your expectations at the right level, and remember that it is your journey, not your friends' or colleagues' journeys. Your journey will not be a straight line; it will be a zigzag. But in the end, you are still climbing toward your North Star. Do not compare your growth to anyone else, and be proud of your journey and your accomplishments. I often say that "I kick ass," meaning I continuously push beyond my comfort zone. You are a shining star, striving to be the best version of yourself!

ACKNOWLEDGMENTS

This book would not be possible without the involvement, understanding, and love of my family. The journey to write this book was extraordinary. Its rich lessons and reflections uncovered my purpose in life. The unconditional support and love of the people around me made this book a reality.

To my dad, Roger, thank you for being the first to enable my personal growth journey. Your support and encouragement mean the world to me. To Agathe, his wife, thank you for sharing and demonstrating your Continuous Improvement journey with all of us.

To my mom, Julie, and my brother, Michel, thank you for listening to my struggles and offering endless encouragement throughout my life. To Robin, Alissandre, and Jean-Pierre, thank you for making me part of one big family and supporting my aspirations.

To my husband, Michael, my soul mate, thank you for keeping me focused on my goal, pushing me to achieve my potential, and for your unconditional love. I would not be where I am without you. To my son, Christophe, thank you for your support in all my endeavors and for always cheering me on. To Bethany, thank you for reading my manuscript and making it better.

To my first readers, Gary Hazen, Nanette Crift, and Jamie Pickett, your ideas and energy improved the book and kept me going. To David Martin, my first official mentor–I did it! To my editor, Kimberly Smith Ashley, I have no words to express the gratitude I have for everything you have done for this book. I'm looking forward to completing the second one with you! Thank you, as well, Joseph Tufano, for taking my words into the stratosphere, and Avery Ashley, for improving all of my grammatical and factual errors. Summer Morris, thank you for translating my vision into the book cover.

BOOKS THAT HELPED MY GROWTH

Here are my favorite books from John C. Maxwell that added great value to me:

1. *Put Your Dream to the Test: 10 Questions to Help You See It and Seize It*

2. *The 21 Irrefutable Laws of Leadership: Follow Them and People Will Follow You*

3. *Today Matters: 12 Daily Practices to Guarantee Tomorrow's Success*

4. *The 15 Invaluable Laws of Growth: Live Them and Reach Your Potential*

5. *Thinking for a Change: 11 Ways Highly Successful People Approach Life and Work*

6. *Developing the Leader Within You 2.0*

7. *The 360° Leader: Developing Your Influence from Anywhere in the Organization*

8. *Everyone Communicates, Few Connect: What the Most Effective People Do Differently*

9. *Leader Shift: The 11 Essential Changes Every Leader Must Embrace*

Here are some other influential books that touched me personally:

1. Brené Brown, *Dare to Lead. Brave work. Tough Conversations. Whole Hearts.*

2. Patty Azzarello, *Rise: 3 Practical Steps for Advancing Your Career, Standing Out as a Leader, and Liking Your Life*

3. The Arbinger Institute, *Leadership and Self-Deception: Getting Out of the Box*

4. The Arbinger Institute, *The Outward Mindset: Seeing Beyond Ourselves*

5. Rachel Hollis, *Girl, Stop Apologizing: A Shame-Free Plan for Embracing and Achieving Your Goals*

Marie-Claude Desrosiers' Destination
Date: October 18, 2015

1. ANALYSIS

All my strengths and my personality profile paint me as an advisor, teacher, and coach to others. I am passionate about CI processes and personal growth.

I spend a lot of time learning about leadership. Connecting with others is important to me and makes me happy. For those reasons, I feel like my purpose is to help others.

2. VISION STORYBOARD

3. YOUR DESTINATION VISION STATEMENT

Write a book about leadership and culture change concepts to help Continuous Improvement professionals succeed.

4. YOUR DESTINATION GOAL

By the end of 2023, my book will add value to at least one million people in the process improvement world.

5. EXISTING GAPS

- I needed to go back to CI. My new role needed to give me experience with leadership concepts around culture change.
- No published book to my name.
- To reach a large number of people, I will need to reach beyond one company. Starting a consultant business would allow me to touch more companies at the same time.

6. YOUR VOYAGES (ACTION PLAN)

VOYAGE #	ACTIVITY NAMES	TARGET DATE
1	Find a job in process improvement.	January 31, 2017
2	Publish a book on the "Leadership concepts of Continuous Improvement."	January 31, 2022
3	Transition from a corporate job to my own consulting firm.	January 31, 2023

Marie-Claude Desrosiers' Voyage #3 - Starting My Own Business
Date: October 18, 2015

1. VOYAGE GOAL AND TIMELINE

By January 1, 2023, I will make the transition from a corporate job to owning my own consulting firm.

2. EXISTING GAPS

- I have never had my own business. To make the same current income, my assumptions and plan are not defined.
- With this new business plan, I may need to sharpen some of my personal skills. I need to identify them, then plan my learnings and practice time to master the new skills.
- Once the book is published and my company created, to get business I will need to promote and market it. Networking is another way to get the word out. No forums exist at this time for me to execute those.
- Any business will need materials to give to clients. These materials need to be created and match the book from voyage #2.

3. ACTION PLAN

ACTION ITEMS	ACTIVITY NAMES	TARGET DATE
1	Create Initial Business Plan	December 31, 2015
PERSONAL GROWTH ACTIVITIES		
2	Improve Speaking Skills	December 31, 2018
3	Improve Coaching Skills	December 31, 2019
4	Improve Selling Skills	December 31, 2020
PROMOTION, NETWORKING AND MARKETING ACTIVITIES		
5	Join Chamber of Commerce and other groups similar in my area	December 31, 2022
6	Create Website and online presence (Facebook)	January 31, 2022
7	Start a Podcast with material from book	July 31, 2022
8	Business Material Activities	December 31, 2022

Marie-Claude believes that personal growth can truly help get you where you need to be. A practitioner of personal growth and continuous improvement for more than twenty years, Marie-Claude has experience in three stages of growth—personal, leadership, and business growth—in which she has trained, mentored, and coached thousands of people to reach their goals, discover their values, and improve their behaviors and processes to become their best selves. She is a certified John Maxwell coach, corporate trainer, and speaker, as well as a women's Life Coach, an Executive Coach for Vice Presidents, and a moderator of better communication for emergent leaders. She currently works for a Top20 Fortune company and lives in Michigan with her family. Learn more about her and her work at www.drivetogrowth.com.

LIFTOFF THOUGHTS

CPSIA information can be obtained
at www.ICGtesting.com
Printed in the USA
BVHW031540141021
618952BV00005B/339/J